LIVING THE

99 THOUGHTS
ON RAISING YOUR PARENTS

Liesl and Max Oestreicher
with Mark Oestreicher

) simply for students

99 Thoughts on Raising Your Parents
Living the Sweet Life at Home

© 2012 Liesl Oestreicher, Max Oestreicher, and Mark Oestreicher

group.com
simplyyouthministry.com

All rights reserved. No part of this book may be reproduced in any manner whatsoever without prior written permission from the publisher, except where noted in the text and in the case of brief quotations embodied in critical articles and reviews. For information, visit group.com/customer-support/permissions.

Credits
Authors: Liesl Oestreicher, Max Oestreicher, and Mark Oestreicher
Executive Developer: Nadim Najm
Chief Creative Officer: Joani Schultz
Editor: Rob Cunningham
Art Director: Veronica Preston

ISBN 978-0-7644-8457-5

10 9 8 7 6 5 4 3 2 1   20 19 18 17 16 15 14 13 12

Printed in the United States of America.

DEDICATION

For our mom, Jeannie Oestreicher, who taught us how to love and be loved.

Start Here I

Communication. 1
Thoughts 1 - 15

Arguments and Disagreements 13
Thoughts 16-28

Understanding Your Parents 21
Thoughts 29-38

Encouraging Your Parents. 29
Thoughts 39-48

School Stuff 37
Thoughts 49-55

Dating. 45
Thoughts 56-62

Rules, Getting Permission, and
Independence 51
Thoughts 63-73

Having Fun. 61
Thoughts 74-83

Friends 69
Thoughts 84-90

Spiritual Life and Church 77
Thoughts 91-99

START HERE

Hi. We're Liesl (18) and Max (14), and we're siblings. We are not made up. We're real teenagers, and we really wrote this book (with a little help from our dad).

You should know this: We're not perfect kids. Not at all.

There are other teenagers (we see them in our church youth groups) who seem more perfect; they seem like the kinds of sons and daughters Christian parents would choose if we were all picked out at a store. Instead, we're two kids who have a good relationship with our parents *and* who aren't perfect. We get in trouble, fight with our parents (and each other), and frustrate our teachers from time to time. In fact, both of us have been sent home from school at one point or another. In other words: We're normal teenagers, and our not-perfect parents are normal, too.

But maybe we're not as normal in this way: We have a really great relationship with our parents. We love them, and they love us. We trust them (most of the time, at least), and they try really, really hard to support us and give us freedom and encouragement. Not that we don't go ballistic with each other from time to time—but even when we do, we're usually pretty good at patching things up.

So our hope is that we can give you a few thoughts (99 of 'em, to be exact) from the perspective of *average* teenagers who have a *better than average* relationship with their parents.

A little more about each of us:

Max
As I write this, I'm in eighth grade, and like most eighth-graders, I'm ready to be out of middle school. I love music; ska, indie-rock, and blues are my favorite genres. I buy as much music as I can afford.

I play drums in the middle school worship band at my church; drums are my main instrument, but I also play ukulele, mandolin, and I'm trying to buy a musical saw (yeah, I like weird instruments). I also drum in a band with two of my friends. We were called Mumbler, but just changed our name to Army of Dave because there's another Mumbler on iTunes® (not that we're on iTunes yet).

I have a slight obsession with bacon. I have tried bacon mints, bacon jelly beans, and bacon soda. I give bacon-related gifts to all my friends for their birthdays. I even have a wallet that looks like it's made out of bacon.

I like pranks. Stink bombs, fake blood, electric shock pens, and stuff set overnight in Jell-O®. My parents are really tired of the smell of stink bombs.

Liesl

As I write this, I will graduate from high school in 9 weeks, 3 days, 3 hours, and 27 minutes. In my opinion, that's way too long. Right after I graduate, I'll work for the summer at an awesome wilderness camp.

Then, next school year, I'm going on a nine-month gap-year trip with a friend. We'll be social and agricultural volunteers in the U.K. and India. When I return, I'll head off to college, in a program that allows me to create my own major. I expect to combine physics or math with music and religious studies.

Like my brother, I'm really into music. My main instrument is viola, but in my church's high school worship band, I play bass guitar and keyboard. I'm also interested in environmentalism, which I express through leading the Planet Team for the high school ministry at my church. Our team collects recyclables to raise money for our sponsor children around the world.

My friends call me a modern-day hippie. I've been a vegetarian for over five years, I have dreadlocks, and I like to sit barefoot at the park, making hemp bracelets and playing acoustic guitar while eating granola. I'm not joking; laugh if you must.

A few more things need to be said before we jump in...

First, with a book this short and in this format (99 thoughts, not a ton of depth on any one subject), we didn't really feel like we had a place to address the super hard stuff that some of you (and some of our friends) have to face. We haven't written about abuse, or neglect, or living with an alcoholic, or any one of dozens of other really difficult situations teenagers find themselves in.

Not including this stuff shouldn't imply that it doesn't matter. Really, it's just the opposite: That stuff matters so much that we didn't want to minimize it by offering two sentences of advice.

If you're in a tough situation like that, please take the risk to find an adult to talk to. Hey, like we said, each of us has a good relationship with our parents, and we've both still found it really important and helpful to talk to other adults at times about problems we're having. We hope you have a youth group leader or someone who's the obvious choice. If you don't have an obvious choice of someone to talk to, pray about who that might be. Look for a safe adult in your church, in your school, or in your neighborhood.

Another thing: Reading over these 99 thoughts, you might sometimes think things are rosier in our family than they are. Actually, things are pretty good at this moment, but they aren't always and haven't always been.

We want to give you a general suggestion we've found to be true: You might go through periods of time—days, weeks, months, even years—when you don't connect well with your parents. You might experience entire seasons where you hardly talk, or where things always seem tense. You might—as we have (Liesl particularly)—feel like there are long periods of time when every conversation leads to disagreement or fighting. Here's what we've learned: Even though it might not feel like it, you have to choose to believe that your parents love you. Even when you're in the lousiest periods of stress and ugliness, when you feel like they totally don't understand you and are being completely unreasonable, hold on to the base truth that their motivation is mostly still trying to figure out what's best for you.

If you can believe that—that they love you and want the best for you—you can weather some of the difficult seasons that most teenagers experience with their parents. At least that's been really helpful for us.

Finally, if you just read these 99 thoughts, you might conclude that we assume every teenager lives with his or her original birth parents. We happen to, but we know you might not. Tons of our friends from church and school don't live with both of their birth parents, and we've seen all kinds of variations: single parents, stepparents, adoptive parents, foster parents, grandparents, or other family members raising teenagers.

When you read the word *parents* in this book, just translate it into your reality. Swap it out, in your mind, for whatever situation you're in, with the adult or adults in your home who are responsible for you.

One more thing: You'll see that at the end of each chapter, we've included a "Stupid Thought." Please know that these are completely sarcastic! Do *not* read them as actual advice, or things will get ugly.

OK, that's about it for now. Let's get on to the 99 thoughts. Thanks for joining us. Keep your hands and feet inside the vehicle, and enjoy the ride!

Liesl and Max

COMMUNICATION

01 TALK IT UP.

You can't have a healthy relationship with your parents if you don't talk to them. Talk about what's going on in your life, how school's going, what's going on in the lives of your friends, and all kinds of other stuff. Sometimes our family will all sit down at the dinner table and share the highs and lows of our day. It gives us a way to talk about stuff we might otherwise forget to mention.

02 LISTEN UP.

Talking is great, but you also have to listen. Ask your parents how their day went. Then listen, and engage with what they say.

03 DON'T IGNORE EMOTIONS.

Emotions are people, too, and no one likes to be ignored (we're kidding, of course, about the first part of that sentence). In order to have successful communication, it's very important to keep your emotions and your parents' emotions in mind.

When I (Liesl) was learning how to drive, my parents and I experienced *lots* of emotions. I was very confident and didn't want to be told I'd done something wrong. On the other hand, my parents were stressing every time I got behind the wheel. It was important for me to keep these elevated emotions in mind when my parents were talking to me about driving skills. If I wasn't careful, I would end up getting defensive, and that would stress them out even more.

04 DON'T ASSUME YOUR PARENTS KNOW THINGS.

Parents aren't mind readers, even if you're afraid they are sometimes. Having them be surprised by something you *thought* they knew, but didn't, can be a frustrating experience for them. So keep them in the know, whether it's your schedule, your reasoning for choices, or your feelings.

05 DON'T ASSUME YOUR PARENTS *DON'T* KNOW THINGS.

Just as the previous assumption can be harmful to great communication, the opposite assumption is also true! But this one isn't so much about constantly bombarding them with all your brilliant insights and ways you can fix them; it's more about not assuming they're stupid.

Sure, most parents can seem completely clueless at times (they are, after all, living in a very different world than we are!)—but that doesn't mean they're idiots.

06 TALK ABOUT THE LITTLE STUFF.

You'll find it super hard to talk about the big stuff—major hurts, huge decisions, big mistakes—if you're not used to talking with your parents at all. So make sure to talk about little things, like the fact that you're having a hard time with a school project, or that you feel bad because you said something hurtful to a friend. If you establish this habit, it won't be so scary to talk about the big stuff.

07 BODY LANGUAGE AND FACIAL EXPRESSIONS ARE A <u>HUGE</u> PART OF COMMUNICATION.

An angry or bored face sometimes communicates more than your words. Same with the way you position your body. So if you want to have good communication with your parents, you have to be aware of your body language and facial expressions during your conversations. It's easy to be completely engaged in your brain but not show it with your body. This can imply something you don't intend and isn't a good setup for successful communication.

08 SECRETS CAN BE DESTRUCTIVE.

Everyone has secrets. We're not suggesting that having a secret makes you a super-sinner or an evil-spawned child. We're just pointing out the reality that secrets can, at times, cause great damage to relationships and communication. But sharing your secrets with your parents can build great bridges of trust.

If you're nervous about sharing something that feels like an emotional risk, just express that: "I'm a little nervous about telling you this, because it's something I haven't told many people."

09 DON'T LIE, BUT IF YOU DO, COME CLEAN.

We heard a statistic that 90 percent of people admit to lying, and the other 10 percent lied when answering the question. Pretty much everybody lies at some point; it's human nature. But that doesn't make it OK. Don't lie to your parents—but if you do, come clean as soon as possible. It's much better to go through the awkwardness (and sometimes the consequences) of admitting you lied, than to have your parents find out you lied without you telling them.

10 LEARN FROM YOUR COMMUNICATION MISTAKES.

So you blew up and made something minor into a really big deal. Or you told a half-truth in an attempt to get what you wanted, and it came back around and bit you in the butt. Pay attention, and don't repeat that mistake next time.

11 NOT ANSWERING IS ANNOYING.

Max here. I'll admit this: I have an annoying habit that drives my parents crazy sometimes (but *only* this one annoying habit—otherwise I am 100 percent pure awesome). I space out and don't respond to their questions. Sometimes I even do this right in the middle of a conversation; like, I'll ask a question, and they'll respond, and I'll just tune out. Usually, I've actually heard what they said, but I just don't think about the need to respond.

Yeah, that's annoying. Don't be like me in that area of communication. Only be like me in all the other areas of my complete awesomeness.

12 SHARE YOUR THOUGHTS.

This whole area of communication with your parents is such a big deal; it can be the difference between a great or lousy experience of living in the same home during your teenage years. But good communication has to be more than sharing logistical information. If all you ever talk about with your parents are the little details of life ("I need to be picked up at 8 p.m.," "I have lots of homework tonight"), then you won't have much of a relationship with your parents. So share your thoughts. Open up and let them know what you're thinking.

13 HAVE MEALS TOGETHER.

Your life and your parents' lives are probably really busy at times. But everyone's gotta eat. So eat dinner together (not in front of the TV). The dinner table is a perfect and natural place to talk to your parents, especially if you all agree to ignore your cell phones for 30 minutes. Our family will often play a card game and talk while we're eating dinner.

14 USE NONSPEAKING WAYS TO TALK TO YOUR PARENTS.

If your parents are anything like ours, they love it when you text them, whether it's info that's helpful for them to know ("I'll be home in a half-hour") or just to thank them for something. Post on their Facebook® pages. Send an email. Or go old school and leave a handwritten note.

These nonspeaking forms of communication can also be super helpful when you're trying to express something (a hurt or frustration), and aren't sure you'll get the words right if you just say it with your mouth.

A word of caution: Don't use these ideas to hide. Don't send a text to tell your parents something huge.

15 GET ADVICE FROM OTHER ADULTS.

Sometimes it's tough to know how your parents will respond. So we've found it's a great idea to get input from another adult. There are plenty of people who would love to have coffee and chat with you: your pastor, a volunteer youth leader, a teacher, an aunt or uncle, or the parent of a friend. Tell them the issue and how you're thinking of sharing it with your parents, then listen to their input. Ask them to keep the conversation confidential until after you've spoken with your parents.

DON'T DO THIS:
SCREAM LOUDER, SO YOUR PARENTS HEAR YOU.

Volume makes all the difference in good communication. So turn it up, baby!

ARGUMENTS AND DISAGREEMENTS

16 TAKE A MINUTE TO BREATHE.

It's super easy to get caught up in your own frustration when you're arguing with your parents. Take a moment, collect yourself, and remember to breathe. I (Liesl) have *really* found this to be a helpful practice.

17 TAKE A BREAK.

Recently, my mom and I (Max) were getting very angry at each other because I wasn't finishing my homework. In the middle of our escalating conversation, I said, "I'm going to take a walk around the block." After returning, my mom and I were all huggy and apologetic.

18 STAY FOCUSED ON THE ISSUE.

When I (Liesl) am annoyed with my parents' opinions, it's common for me to attack the person rather than staying focused on the issue. This may be easier and can feel right in the short run, but it ends up making that person feel disrespected or hurt.

First, this approach is mean, so stop it! Second, when your parents feel disrespected, they're way less likely to see your perspective.

19 PICK YOUR BATTLES.

Don't start an argument over something stupid. If you suggest pizza for dinner, and your mom says no, you're dumber than a sheep if you turn it into World War III.

20 PAY ATTENTION TO YOUR TONE.

There are three parts to communication, and they're all equally important when trying to survive a disagreement: words, body language, and tone. Tone is that part of your communication that can make "Yeah, you're right" mean either "Yes, I admit that you are correct" or "You are such an idiot!"

My parents (Liesl here) totally think I'm defensive regularly, when I'm actually not, just because of the tone in my voice. We haven't figured this out yet, and it's annoying to all of us.

21 DON'T EXAGGERATE.

Saying things like "You never..." and "You always..." won't help your case. They just make you sound like a kid.

22 KEEP EMOTIONS FROM ESCALATING.

Once disagreements get loud in volume and intense with emotion, very little can be accomplished. So as much as you can, try to chill. It's in your best interest.

23 WORK TO UNDERSTAND YOUR PARENTS' POINT OF VIEW.

If your only goal is to win an argument, then the other person's point of view doesn't really matter. But if you can at least admit that your parents are *sometimes* right (a pretty healthy perspective in life, by the way), then you've got to work to try to understand what's behind their opinion.

24 BE WILLING TO ADMIT YOU'RE WRONG.

Sometimes in the middle of an argument, I (Max) realize I'm wrong, but I keep charging ahead because I don't want to admit my error. That's lame. You have to admit that your parents are right (when they are!), if you ever hope to have them admit you're right.

25 BE HUMBLE WHEN YOU'RE RIGHT.

The only thing worse than a sore loser is an arrogant winner. Don't be that guy (or girl).

26 DIFFERENCE OF OPINIONS DOESN'T ALWAYS MEAN SOMEONE'S WRONG.

We usually assume there's only one correct point of view, like it's a winner-take-all competition. But this is rarely the case, and there's usually some amount of truth on both sides. And it's possible that *both* opinions are fine and good, just different.

27 SEEK A COMPROMISE.

It's really hard to completely talk your parent out of his or her opinion. But if you're willing to compromise your position, your parent may be willing to compromise, too.

28 PRAY.

It would be awesome if God would help bring understanding and resolution to arguments between you and your parents, right? Well, the good news is that God *wants* to help. So ask!

DON'T DO THIS:
MAKE SURE YOU ALWAYS WIN.

The best result isn't nearly as important as winning! If you always win your arguments, your parents will respect you.

ARGUMENTS AND DISAGREEMENTS

UNDERSTANDING YOUR PARENTS

29 PARENTING IS HARD.

It's easy to forget this one. But seriously, can you imagine how difficult it must be to figure *you* out? And how difficult it must be to set the right boundaries and encourage you in the right ways? Cut your parents some slack, man!

30 PARENTS SOMETIMES HAVEN'T HAD GOOD EXAMPLES TO FOLLOW.

Maybe your grandparents were *amazing* parents. But it's doubtful they were perfect. And what if they were less than amazing? Can you imagine how hard it would be to figure out parenting if your parents' parents had been mean or angry or abusive? This parenting thing must feel like a road trip without a map at times.

31 PARENTS ARE AFRAID THEIR PARENTING STINKS.

Not all parents will admit this, but if they're really honest, most parents feel, from time to time, that they're doing a lousy job. They're afraid they're screwing up. They're afraid we're going to end up hating them or needing years and years of therapy because of their inadequacies. We're not suggesting you should pretend everything's peachy if it's not, but it's probably fair to say that the God-pleasing thing would be to show some sensitivity and toss them a bone of praise once in a while.

32 PARENTS ARE UNDER LOTS OF EXTERNAL PRESSURE.

It seems like so many people feel the need to coach parents, letting them know what they're doing wrong. Some of the stupid things our parents do are because of social norms and expectations. Your parents might feel that if they ever go against these norms, their parenting is automatically deemed insufficient.

33 PARENTS HAVE LOTS OF RESPONSIBILITIES.

The two of us have pretty cool parents, really—but they both get stressed out from all the responsibilities in their lives. Our mom's a full-time grad student, and our dad works hard to run his own little business. They're both really busy and have lots of demands on their lives. In the midst of all that, they try really hard to stay engaged in our lives and meet our needs. It's important for us to keep this in mind, and realize that the world doesn't revolve around us.

34 DON'T ASSUME YOU KNOW THEIR MOTIVATION.

This is a good principle to live by with anyone, not just your parents. But since you know your parents so well, it's an easy mistake to make. Assuming you know their motivation (particularly if you assume it's a bad motivation) can quickly lead you to conclusions that are completely wrong. Like, if your parents have a rule for you that seems totally unfair, you might assume that they created it because they don't want you to grow up. But maybe their motivation is more about giving you freedom within a boundary they think you can handle.

For example, when my parents (Max here) wanted me to text them where I was when I was walking around our town with a friend, I thought they weren't ready to let me have that freedom. But when we talked about it, I found out their reason was just the opposite: They actually wanted me to have freedom, but in a safe way.

35 THEY ONLY WANT WHAT'S BEST FOR YOU.

We know this sounds cliché, but it's true (most of the time).

36 THEY WERE OUR AGE ONCE.

It's weird to think about, but your parents went through some of the same stuff you go through. Even though they're old now, they probably understand more about being a teenager than you think they do. So ask them for advice. And you might try this thing that the two of us like to do: We ask our parents to tell stories from their own teenage years.

37 YOUR PARENTS CAN'T MEET ALL YOUR NEEDS.

Parents are humans, too, and they don't have the means of meeting some of your deepest needs. Don't blame them. Turn instead to God, who knows you and loves you even more than your parents do. And God *does* have the means to meet your deepest needs!

38 YOU AND YOUR PARENTS ARE GOD'S GIFTS TO EACH OTHER.

God paired you up with your parents for a reason. Not only can you learn from them, they also can learn from you.

DON'T DO THIS:
MAKING PARENTING EVEN HARDER FOR YOUR PARENTS IS GOOD FOR THEM.

We all grow best when we go through tough times, so give your parents the gift of growth by making it really difficult for them!

ENCOURAGING YOUR PARENTS

39 SHOW YOUR PARENTS YOU CARE ABOUT THEM.

This seems obvious, but we know so many teenagers who never live this out. If you struggle with this one, then think about it this way: Your life will be *so much better* if your parents know you care about them!

40 SAY NICE THINGS.

This sounds like a greeting card or something your grandma would have cross-stitched in her bathroom. But it really is a game-changer for parent/teen relationships. A random kind word covers up for a bunch of the stupid things you probably say. (We write this from experience!)

41 SHOW INTEREST IN THEIR LIVES.

Do you really understand your mom's job? Do you actually know how your dad spends his day? The simple act of asking your parents about their lives communicates truckloads of encouragement. Of course, you can't just ask: You have to show that you really want to hear the answer.

42 LET THEM KNOW THAT THEIR INTERESTS MATTER, TOO.

It's not all about you! Sometimes you *and* your parents don't remember that. They can get so caught up in raising you that they forget about themselves. Your parents have dreams and aspirations, too. So let them know that they're important and that you'd love to see them go for it.

When our mom started grad school a couple of years ago, I (Liesl) wrote her a letter, telling her how proud I was that she was achieving a dream of hers. I told her how inspiring it was for me to see her work hard for something she wanted in her life. She still has my note taped to her desk where she studies.

43 YOU'RE *NOT* TOO OLD FOR PHYSICAL AFFECTION.

Sure, you might not want to hold hands with your dad while you're walking through a mall! But there's still a time and place for physical affection with your parents—even if it's just a hug, or a hand on their shoulder. Touch has a huge impact. So get over the awkwardness and bring on the love.

44 VERBALIZE YOUR DESIRE TO GROW SPIRITUALLY.

Your parents work really hard to help you grow into a responsible and motivated Christ-follower. Let them know that you share this desire for your life and that all their effort isn't going to waste.

45 GIVE THOUGHTFUL GIFTS.

Everyone gives Christmas and birthday gifts, plus stuff at times like Mother's Day and Father's Day. Parents don't care about the price of the gift, as much as they care about the thought and time you put into it. Parents would generally rather receive a handmade card with an encouraging letter in it than a $20 Starbucks® gift card. Sentimental wins over expensive every time.

46 INITIATE SPENDING TIME WITH YOUR PARENTS.

There's probably nothing that makes our parents happier than when we suggest doing something together. I (Max) love asking my dad to go to movies together, and asking my mom to go for a hike. I (Liesl) find that my mom is stoked when I ask her if the two of us can go to dinner together, and my dad gets a cheesy grin on his face when I ask him if we can chill in the backyard and chat.

47 SHOW APPRECIATION FOR LITTLE THINGS.

It's one thing to thank your parents for a big Christmas gift, or some other major thing. But you might be surprised by how encouraged your parents are when you thank them for little things, like a ride to a friend's house, or lunch packed for school. The practice of thankfulness could completely change the vibe of your home. Of course, make sure you actually mean it!

48 SHARE YOUR HOPES, DREAMS, AND FEARS.

Even if you never say it, only sharing shallow information with your parents gives them the impression that you don't trust them. So get risky and share the deeper stuff of your life. You'll end up communicating that you trust your parents, and that will come back to you in lots of great ways.

DON'T DO THIS:
POINT OUT ALL YOUR PARENTS' FLAWS, CONSTANTLY.

Your parents have lots of flaws, and it's your responsibility to point out every single one of them, as often as possible. God wants your parents to be humble, and this will help!

SCHOOL STUFF

49 KEEP YOUR PARENTS INFORMED.

Both of us are decent students. But we've both had bumps in the road, for sure. And we can tell you from experience that our parents absolutely hate it when they get blindsided by a bad progress report or news of a missed deadline. Because school work and grades are one of the biggest sources of tension between parents and teenagers, it's *always* a good idea to give your parents a heads-up of what's going on, particularly if it's less than spiffy.

50 ASK FOR HELP.

You know and we know that school and homework is pretty much our *job* at this point in our lives. And maybe your mom isn't going to teach you calculus. But asking for help has a double benefit: First—obviously— you might actually get help. Second, it can become time spent together, and that's always an opportunity for strengthening your relationship.

51 ARTICULATE YOUR NEEDS AND WHAT'S NOT HELPFUL.

I (Liesl) was having all kinds of tension with my mom and dad early last year (my junior year) over homework. They wanted me to take responsibility but didn't like how I was handling that. It caused us to get into fights way too many times. Eventually, my mom decided she didn't want to keep guessing how to help, when it was annoying both of us so much. So she actually put the responsibility on me: Tell her what I needed from her, and what I didn't need. I was super specific about the few areas where I wanted help (ask me what I have to get done, don't let me turn on the TV on weekdays until my work is done), and also what I didn't need (nagging!). It's been way more helpful for both of us, and this year feels totally different.

52 DISCUSS GOALS.

If you want to succeed at school, it's really helpful to set goals. Your parents can be awesome in this area, because they have to set goals all the time in life. They can give input on what goals are realistic, and keep you on track toward achieving them.

53 MORE RESPONSIBILITY SHOWN = MORE INDEPENDENCE GIVEN.

If you're more responsible with your schoolwork, you'll experience a massive overflow effect: Your parents will give you more freedom in other areas of your life. It's not just a reward thing. It's that they will be more convinced you can handle the extra freedom without being an idiot.

54 SHARE WHAT YOU ENJOY.

It's easy to complain about school, only telling your parents what you don't like. Telling them that negative stuff is OK, but try to verbalize positive stuff, too. Even if you don't like *any* of your classes, you can find *something* to be positive about!

55 TALK ABOUT YOUR FUTURE.

If your parents don't know your dreams, how can you expect them to not accidentally get in the way of your dreams? Talk to them about what you want for your future, and ask them to help you think about the steps you need to take. (This is where their greater life experience can come in really handy!) I (Liesl) am getting ready for college, and it's crazy and overwhelming at times. I can't imagine getting it all done if my parents weren't helping me.

DON'T DO THIS:
HIDE YOUR REPORT CARD!

If you're worried about getting in trouble because of a bad report card, don't fret. Hide it, and your parents will never know!

DATING

56 TALK IT THROUGH.

For most teenagers, talking about crushes and likes and dating and sex and everything else in this bucket of subjects is incredibly awkward. But you have to choose to go there. Tell your parents that you'd rather the whole subject *not* be weird for all of you. Find out what they're thinking. C'mon, dive into the awkwardness!

57 PARENTS ARE FREAKED.

If you've dated at all, you've likely experienced this. While they might think an innocent little date is "cute" (annoying, right?), deep down most of them are worried that you're going to mess up your whole life, either by getting serious with a total loser or by something huge like getting pregnant (or getting someone else pregnant). So if your parents act a bit weird sometimes (most of the time?) when the subject of dating comes up, remember that it's usually because they're concerned you're going to get hurt.

58 REALIZE YOU'RE THEIR BABY.

Yeah, that sounds cheesy. But think of it this way: It was *really recently*, from your parents' perspective, that you were a kid. So the idea of you *dating* is, like, seriously weird!

59 THEY MIGHT HAVE GOOD ADVICE FOR YOU.

We've written this thought in a few of these categories, but it's really worth mentioning here also. In most cases, your parents will have more experience than you in all things dating: defining the relationship, breaking up, appropriate gifts, and all kinds of other stuff. But you won't get input unless you tell 'em what's going on and ask for help.

60 KNOW YOUR PARENTS' BOUNDARIES.

If you don't know what your parents' dating boundaries are for you, ask. It's totally possible that they've never really thought this through, and it could generate an important dialogue for both of you (by the way, this is a good time to ask about their own experiences). You'll still have to make the choice whether you're going to stick to their boundaries, but you can't do that unless you know what they are.

61 DON'T LIE ABOUT THE REALITIES OF A RELATIONSHIP.

Trust is essential to establishing a good relationship with your parents. So many teenagers lie to their parents about dating, and you're going to have to pick a lane: honesty or lies. If you head down the road of lying all the time, it will only come back to bite you in the booty.

62 BE HONEST ABOUT UNHELPFUL REACTIONS.

If you tell your parents about a girl or a guy you have feelings for, they might respond with something like, "Ooh, that's so cute." No one likes that. Be honest and tell them that response isn't helpful and that you don't like it.

DON'T DO THIS:
CREATE A FAKE BOYFRIEND OR GIRLFRIEND.

If you really want to earn your parents' respect, make up a super impressive, convincing, and wholesome love interest. Just make sure your parents don't invite your "date" over for dinner.

RULES, GETTING PERMISSION, AND INDEPENDENCE

63 HONESTY LEADS TO INDEPENDENCE.

It's hard to write this suggestion without sounding like parents ourselves. It's the kind of thing you hear from parents, right? But that doesn't mean it's not true—just the opposite. If you want to have freedom and independence, your parents have to know that they can trust you to be honest with them. If they know (or sense) that you lie to them all the time, you're damaging their trust, which means you're decreasing the odds that your parents will give you more freedom. We've found that honesty, even when it leads to short-term frustration or restrictions, generally leads to more permission in the long run.

64 TRUSTWORTHINESS LEADS TO INDEPENDENCE.

This suggestion is kinda like the last one, but broader. Being honest is a part of being trustworthy, but trustworthiness is bigger than honesty. Being trustworthy means—obviously!—being worthy of trust. Being worthy of trust means you've proven yourself. For example, if your parents trust you with something little, like finishing your homework before you watch TV, you have a chance to prove yourself trustworthy or untrustworthy. The more you prove yourself trustworthy, the more your parents will give you freedom and independence. So even if you don't feel like making a choice that your parents would want you to make, think of it as an investment in your future freedom.

65 IF THE ANSWER IS NO, ASK HOW TO GET TO YES.

Your parents usually have legitimate reasons for setting rules, even if it doesn't seem like it. Sometimes there's something in the way of them giving you permission. If you ask them what that thing is, you may be able to work toward changing their no to a yes. Maybe they think you're too young, and you just need to wait a few years. Maybe they feel like you need to earn more of their trust, and you can talk about how to do that. Or maybe it's something as simple as them wanting you to finish that history paper before doing something social. Trust us: It doesn't hurt to ask.

66 IF RULES AREN'T CLEAR, ASK.

We know it seems easier to ask for forgiveness than to ask for permission, but that's not a good way to get more independence. If you don't understand the specifics of a rule, ask for clarification.

67 SUGGEST A TRIAL PERIOD.

If you ask your parents if you can do something and they're skeptical, chances are good that they'll say, "We need to talk about it," or "No." So ask for a trial period: Ask if they'll let you try it once, or for a period of time, then come back together to evaluate.

68 SUGGEST BOUNDARIES, OR THEY'LL BE SET FOR YOU.

Taking initiative with your own rules is a great way to show responsibility, and your parents are more likely to give you what you want. For example, when I (Liesl) want to borrow the car for a night to stay at a friend's house, my parents will feel better about it if I tell them my whole plan. And it's more likely that I'll get permission than if I just leave it to them to set the boundaries. I might say something like, "I will home by 9 a.m., I will contribute gas money, and I will update you on where I am throughout the night."

69 REMEMBER THE SPIRIT OF THE LAW, NOT JUST THE LETTER OF THE LAW.

In case you don't know what that means: The "letter of the law" means the actual rule, like "finish your homework before turning on the TV." But there are always gray areas and ways to bend the rules, right? The "spirit of the law" means the intent behind the rule. Let's say you do the bare minimum of your homework, taking shortcuts and generally blowing it off. Then, when you're sitting in front of the TV and your mom asks you about your homework, you might be able to semi-honestly say you finished, but you really didn't follow the spirit of the law. And if your parents find out, things get messy, and they'll often add more rules (which you don't want, right?).

70 DON'T ALWAYS EXPECT AN IMMEDIATE ANSWER.

Your parents aren't computers, and sometimes they need extra processing time. If you're asking permission for something, it's not always in your best interest to push for an immediate answer. If they need time to think, let them (though it's fair to ask how long they need, so it doesn't get left open indefinitely). If you push for an immediate answer, you might corner your parents into giving the response you don't want.

71 BE AWARE OF MOOD AND CIRCUMSTANCES.

If I (Max) ask my dad, "Can I buy this album?" when he is on the phone and stressed out, he's probably going to say no. But if ask the same question when he's watching TV and happy, he's more likely to say yes. Be smart about your timing.

72 DON'T WHINE.

If your parents give you an answer you don't want to hear, don't whine. It's not going to help, and it might even make the situation worse. Whining just makes you seem immature.

73 SMILEY HAPPY FACE WORKS BETTER THAN POUTY PUPPY DOG FACE.

You're not as cute as you think you are when you stick out your bottom lip and talk in a baby voice. Trust us. Smiling and using a confident tone will show your parents that you are mature and will not annoy them like pouting will. You're also more likely to bring your parents over to your side.

DON'T DO THIS:
SUCK UP.

Bake a batch of brownies. Say, "I love you." Give a head massage. Whatever it takes, use flattery and bribery to get what you want!

HAVING FUN

74 ENGAGE.

Here's the deal: You can't have fun with your parents if you don't pay attention. In other words, it's lame to tune out (or pop in earbuds, or focus on your cell and texts) when you're hanging out with your parents. They'll quickly get annoyed or bored, and you'll lose out as much as them. We know it's difficult, but there are times when you just gotta put the cell phone away.

75 LET THEM KNOW WHEN YOU'RE HAVING FUN.

Most of us teenagers have a natural tendency to look the part of a rebellious, angst-filled kid. Sometimes, even if we're having a great time, we can't help but fold our arms, slouch in our chair, and roll our eyes. To our parents, this says we're not having fun. So be intentional about how you present yourself in these situations. Sit up, uncross your arms, and look engaged. You can even verbally let them know you're having a great time. Even though it seems like such a little thing that shouldn't matter much, your parents will appreciate it.

76 SO WHAT IF THEY'RE DORKS?

We can guarantee that you are just as much of a dork—if not more so—than your parents. So don't be hatin'! Maybe your parents do sing really loud in public (like our mom does). Or maybe they try to make your friends laugh by telling really bad jokes (like our dad does). But do you really want them to act old and boring? Sing with your mom, and laugh at your dad's jokes! You might all look like dorks together, but you'll be having fun while doing so.

77 DON'T BUY THE LIE THAT IT'S LAME TO HANG OUT WITH YOUR PARENTS.

There's a constant message to teenagers in our world that parents are lame, stupid, clueless, and annoying. And sometimes our parents do things that *are* lame, stupid, clueless, or annoying. But even if (or when) that's true, it doesn't mean it's lame to hang out with them. Our mom and dad can be complete freaks at times, but we still choose to hang out with them. This isn't just because we're being nice—our lives are actually better because we choose to hang out with our parents.

78 GAME NIGHT.

Just saying "game night" sounds cheesy to me (Max), but it can be a great way to hang out and laugh together. Our favorite family games are Dominoes, Texas Hold 'Em Poker, Uno®, and an awesome card game called Monopoly® Deal (seriously, find it; you will thank us). This is fun with just your family, or a great way to let your parents and friends get to know each other.

79 COOK A MEAL TOGETHER.

Often we think of mealtime as an opportunity for family bonding. But you can also take advantage of the time it takes to prepare the meal. We have an Oestreicher family vacation tradition where each of us will take charge of a meal. The whole family cooks each person's menu together, and we have a great time.

80 MAKE FUN A REGULAR THING.

Hanging out with your parents on vacation is great, but try to make fun a regular thing—like, at breakfast or dinner, on car rides, or during lazy weekends.

81 TRY NEW THINGS TOGETHER.

Some of the most fun we ever have with our parents is when we're all trying something new together. It makes us all rookies, and there's fun in that.

As we write this section, we're on a vacation in the mountains of Washington, and yesterday our family hiked a very remote and hard-to-follow trail. We had to help each other cross a river (on a log), find the trail, and move branches out of the way for each other. But the whole thing created a fantastic memory of a shared experience.

82 DO SOMETHING YOUR PARENTS THINK IS FUN.

This suggestion is a bit of a stretch, because it crosses into the idea of putting your parents' needs and desires over your own (clearly, not an easy thing). We normally think of fun times with our parents in terms of the stuff *we* think is fun. But it's a good and healthy thing to sometimes think of stuff *they* think is fun. You might not have as much fun with the activity itself, but you can find fun in time with your parents and in their enjoyment of what you're doing together.

Because most parents are so used to putting our needs in front of their own, they won't think this way. So you might need to ask, "What would *you* find fun?"

83 TAKE ADVANTAGE OF SCHOOL BREAKS.

We know that on school breaks, you might want to be lazy and hang out with friends, but days off school are a perfect time to hang out with your parents. It's not like it's bad to hang with your friends or be lazy on break, but also try to do something with your mom or dad. It doesn't have to be elaborate—just spend time together.

DON'T DO THIS:
MOCK EACH OTHER.

Mocking your parents is great, especially if you hurt their feelings. It might make them sad, but you'll be having fun!

FRIENDS

84 LET YOUR PARENTS GET TO KNOW YOUR FRIENDS.

We teenagers have a tendency to keep our friend world separate from our family world. While that's understandable, it's not always the best way to build trust with your parents (which, remember, helps you get more freedom and independence). Try to find times when you can include your friends with your family, or your parents with your friends. I (Liesl) sometimes like including my friends at our family dinners. My parents are nice to my friends, and it helps my parents be less nervous when I want to hang out with those friends.

85 TELL YOUR PARENTS GOOD THINGS YOUR FRIENDS DO.

Along the same lines as the last thought, help your parents know what's great about your friends. If your friend wins an award, does well at a sports event, gets a role in a play, or simply does something nice or brave, tell your parents. It helps your parents get to know your friends better and puts them in a positive light. This isn't about manipulating your parents; it's about helping them know the good stuff you're already aware of.

86 SHARE WHAT YOU LIKE ABOUT YOUR FRIENDS.

Your parents will always trust you more if they know your motivations—why you do the things you do and choose the things you choose. The same is true when it comes to friends. If you want your parents to trust you with your buds (especially if they don't know those friends), help them understand why you're choosing to hang out with that person. Maybe it's because you like the same things, or you admire something about them. Maybe it's because they make you laugh, or they help you with your problems. Sharing these reasons will also help you think about why you like your friends, which is a nice little bonus.

87 TRY NOT TO RIP ON YOUR PARENTS TO YOUR FRIENDS.

It's OK to vent to one or two of your friends about your parents, but don't tell everyone that your parents stink. How would you like it if your parents told everyone that you're a terrible child? Besides, constantly bagging on your parents doesn't exactly help your own outlook about them.

88 ASK FOR ADVICE ABOUT FRIENDS.

Your parents have lived longer than you and probably have good insight when you're not getting along with a friend. It's often helpful to get a third party's point of view. And it's awesome for your parents to know that you trust them with this kind of information. Just the other day, I (Liesl) was having major drama with a couple of my friends, and talking to my mom about it helped ease my stress and sort through the details.

89 ASK FOR ADVICE *FOR* YOUR FRIENDS.

I (Liesl) have a natural instinct to help out my friends. But some of the challenges my friends go through are not things I know how to fix. My parents are great at giving input. First of all, they have more life experience, which usually makes them more qualified to solve scary situations. And they're not as emotionally involved in my friends' lives, which can make it easier to see the situation clearly. You can even keep things confidential: Just tell your parents that you don't think it's your place to give your friends' secrets away, and then ask them for input without using a name.

90 ASK YOUR FRIENDS FOR ADVICE ABOUT YOUR PARENTS.

Most teenagers go through similar, if not identical, problems. If you're having trouble at home, ask your friends what they would do. This is helpful in a couple of ways. Your friends may have some seriously good advice. Also, the simple act of describing the situation can give you insight.

DON'T DO THIS:
KEEP YOUR PARENTS INFORMED BY ALWAYS INCLUDING THEM IN EVERY ACTIVITY YOU DO WITH YOUR FRIENDS.

Whatever you do with your friends is an opportunity to also hang out with your parents. Wrestling, sleepovers, video gaming, pranking, shopping, school dances... EVERYTHING! That way, you might end up with no friends, which just means more time with Mom and Dad!

SPIRITUAL LIFE AND CHURCH

91 INVOLVE YOUR PARENTS IN YOUR SPIRITUAL CURIOSITY.

It's good to ask questions. Involving your parents in your spiritual questioning might seem scary at first, but it will actually show them that you're being intentional about your beliefs.

Plus, talking to your parents about your spiritual questions can help you move closer to a conclusion. This may also help your parents' spirituality; they may not have thought of the questions you come up with.

92 ASK TO HEAR YOUR PARENTS' SPIRITUAL JOURNEY.

Some parents feel funny telling their teenagers about their own story. They wonder if their kids will be bored, or if their struggles will *make* their kids have struggles. So sometimes, parents just need permission to share—they need to know you want to hear how they came to believe what they believe. Ask them about the times they've wrestled with doubts and questions. Because you know them so well, hearing this part of their lives can be super helpful in your own spiritual journey.

93 SHARE WHAT WAS DISCUSSED AT CHURCH.

Tell your parents what was discussed in youth group, small group, or Sunday school. Or if you attend the same church service as your parents, just bring up the sermon. Get your parents' point of view on the stories or topics, and wrestle with them together. This is helpful for you and for them, because it builds your relationship with your parents while helping all of you think about what you heard and learned.

94 PRAY TOGETHER.

Our family definitely forgets sometimes, but it's great to pray together, really engaging in the prayer. When I (Max) was little, and was asked to pray for dinner, I would say, "Thank you God, for this food, amen," as fast as I possibly could. Don't do that. Don't rush it; really focus on the prayer, and have more than one person pray to create one mega-prayer! Praying together does amazing things to bond a family.

Mix it up also. Try different ways of praying together: Share prayer requests, pray Scripture, sing worship songs as prayer, focus on thanks, or try one-word prayers.

95 SIT TOGETHER IN CHURCH.

In your church, you might have services where adults and teenagers are all in the service together. If that's your situation, don't always sit with your friends, far away from your parents. At least some of the time, sit with your parents and share the spiritual experience of worshipping side by side.

96 FAMILY GIVING.

We have a really cool tradition in our family called The Jesus Gift. Each Christmas, our parents give us a "multiplier" amount, like 10x or 20x. The two of us put our own money in, and our parents match our donation by the multiplier amount. So if the two of us put in $50, and our parents are matching it by 10x, then they'll add $500. Then the two of us get to decide who to donate the money to, from our family.

We've also all set up accounts with Kiva, an organization that makes microloans to people in the developing world who are trying to get businesses going. This started when our parents gave us money in a Kiva account (kiva.com) as part of a Christmas gift. But we all enjoy telling each other what and who we're loaning funds to.

These "family giving" practices have been really cool for us, helping us remember to share God's love with the world in practical ways.

97 DON'T BELIEVE SOMETHING JUST BECAUSE YOUR PARENTS DO, BUT DON'T REJECT BELIEFS JUST BECAUSE YOUR PARENTS BELIEVE THEM.

It's really important that you form your own faith, rather than just adopting your parents' beliefs. But this isn't to say that you shouldn't believe something just because they do! It's crucial that you know what resonates with you and what doesn't, and it's OK if those things aren't always the same as your parents. In short: Don't be a nonthinker, but don't be a rebel either.

98 SERVE OTHERS WITH YOUR PARENTS.

We'll be honest: We don't do this often enough. But when we *have* served other people together as a family, it's been super meaningful. A few things we've done together: We volunteered together at a homeless feeding program in our city a few times, we helped sort donated food at a Salvation Army warehouse, and we've taken a couple of day trips to Mexico (we live 20 minutes away!) to serve people there. There's something really awesome about being together while we're getting the focus off of ourselves and onto the needs of other people.

99 DEVELOP SPIRITUAL FAMILY TRADITIONS FOR CHRISTIAN HOLIDAYS.

We told you about our Jesus Gift tradition at Christmas, but we have a few other spiritual family traditions that are meaningful to us

SPIRITUAL LIFE AND CHURCH

and pull us together as a family. For years on Easter weekend, we have created a holy space, with a cross, covering it with a dark cloth on Good Friday and removing the cloth on Easter morning. We read the whole Easter story from the Bible, and each person draws a picture representing a part of the story (or our response to it). Then we tape up all the pictures from all the years we've done this, in the order they unfold in the story, and prayerfully walk through the whole thing.

At Thanksgiving, we have a tradition of sharing things we're thankful for before we eat.

You can create your own family traditions along these same lines. Exactly what you do isn't as important as doing something. When you repeat these traditions each year, they become more and more meaningful to your family, and remind you all of your connection to each other and Jesus.

DON'T DO THIS:
KEEP YOUR FAITH TO YOURSELF (THEY DON'T WANT TO HEAR ABOUT IT).

Make sure you don't talk about your faith with your parents. We can promise you that they really don't care at all about your spiritual needs.

SPIRITUAL LIFE AND CHURCH